Art & Activities for Kids

Make Clothes Fun!

Kim Solga

NORTH LIGHT BOOKS

Cincinnati, Ohio

96 95 94 93 92   5 4 3 2 1

Library of Congress Cataloging in Publication Data

Solga, Kim.
   Make clothes fun! / Kim Solga.
      p.   cm. – (Art & activities for kids)
   Summary: Ten projects involving the decoration of clothing using paints and other household materials, resulting in such creations as painted T-shirts, cloth collages, and jazzed-up denim jackets.
      ISBN 0-89134-421-7
   1. Handicraft – Juvenile literature. 2. Wearable art – Juvenile literature. [1. Handicraft. 2. Clothing and dress.] I. Title. II. Series.
TT160.S585   1991
746.9'2 – dc20   91-38802
                                                          CIP
                                                           AC

Edited by Julie Wesling Whaley
Design Direction by Clare Finney
Art Direction by Kristi Kane Cullen
Photography by Pamela Monfort
Very special thanks to Theresa Brockman, Marilyn A. Daiker, Kitty Denny, Shelley Edelschick, Kelly Jackson, Jeremy Reiber, Christa Russell, Kathy Savage-Hubbard, Niki Smith, Tina Westerkamp, Suzanne Whitaker, and the kids of Sisson School in Mt. Shasta, California.

Make Clothes Fun! features ten unique and diverse projects, plus numerous variations, for decorating clothing. These projects will fire the imaginations of girls and boys aged six to eleven. They are open-ended: kids learn techniques they can use to decorate clothes according to their own designs. The emphasis is on fun. Kids will love working with fabrics and fabric paint, sewing, weaving, embroidering, tie-dyeing, decorating with materials from buttons to lace to studs, and designing caps and team insignia patches.

By inviting kids to try new things, *Make Clothes Fun!* encourages individual creativity. In addition to learning artistic skills, children will use fine motor and problem-solving skills to produce beautiful garments to wear or give away. Young "clothing designers" will beam when someone admires a garment they've made or decorated themselves. All the projects are kid-tested to ensure success and inspire confidence.

Getting the Most out of the Projects

While the projects provide clear step-by-step instructions and photographs, children should feel free to substitute and improvise. Some of the projects are easy to do in a short amount of time. Others require more patience, and even adult supervision. The symbols on page 6 will help you recognize the more challenging activities.

The list of materials shown at the beginning of each activity is for the featured project only.

Suggested alternatives may require different supplies. Again, children are encouraged to substitute and use whatever materials they have access to (and permission to use!). The projects offer flexibility to make it easy for you and your child to try as many activities as you wish.

Safety

The activities in this book were developed for the enjoyment of children. We've taken every precaution to ensure their safety and success. Please follow the directions and note where an adult's help is required, especially when children are using paints and markers that are not specifically labeled "nontoxic." In fact, feel free to work alongside your young artists as often as you can. They will appreciate help in reading and learning new techniques, and will love the chance to talk with you and show off their creations. Children thrive on attention and praise, and craft adventures are the perfect setting for both.

Collecting Supplies

All of the projects can be done with household items or inexpensive, easy-to-find supplies (see page 7 for definitions of any craft materials you're not already familiar with). Here are some household items you'll want to make sure you have on hand: newspapers, scrap paper and cloth, ribbons, lace, yarn, buttons, leftover latex housepaint, soda straws, felt, beads, paper clips, string, rubber bands, safety pins, rubber gloves, plastic utensils, bucket and sponges.

Be a Good Artist

Work Habits

Get permission to work at your chosen workspace before you begin. Cover your workspace with newspapers or a vinyl tablecloth.

Wear a smock or big, old shirt to protect the clothes you wear while you're painting, using dye, or decorating other clothes.

Always get permission before you decorate any clothes. Practice on scrap paper or old clothes before working on good clothes. Work slowly and carefully.

If you decorate new clothes, wash and dry them before you begin. Put wax paper between layers of cloth so the paint or dye won't "bleed" through to the back.

Follow the directions carefully for each project. When you see the adult and child symbol, have an adult help you.

Don't put art materials in your mouth. If you're working with a younger child, don't let him put art materials in his mouth, either.

The clock symbol means you must wait to let something dry before going on to the next step. It is very important not to rush ahead.

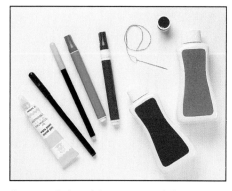

Some of the things you might use to make clothes fun, like permanent markers and dye, could be harmful, so *always get an adult to help you.*

Always finish by cleaning your workspace and all your tools.

Craft Materials

Use a **ruler** to measure the pieces you need. This symbol, ", means inches—12" means twelve inches; cm means centimeters (3 cm equals about 1"). This symbol, ', means feet—3' means 3 feet; m means meter (3' equals about 1 m).

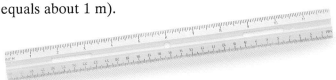

Fabric is another word for cloth. For most of the projects in this book, natural fabric such as cotton will work better than synthetic fabric like polyester. Experiment on scraps before you work on good clothes.

A *garment* is something you wear, like a shirt, jacket, cap or shoes. You can decorate almost any garment to make it special.

A *seam* is the line where two pieces of fabric are sewn together. You'll make seams in Towel Tops (page 32) and decorate seams in Jacket Jazz (page 38). A *hem* is found along the bottom of a garment, where the fabric is turned under to make a smooth edge (see page 37). There's more on how to sew on page 32.

Scissors. Scissors need to be sharp to cut through fabric. Be careful when you cut with them. Test different scissors in your house until you find a pair that will cut cloth easily. If you buy a new pair just for fabric, mark them "Sewing" and don't use them for paper. That way, they'll stay sharp longer.

Pinking shears are a special scissors that cut a zigzag line. Cutting with them will help keep the cut edge from fraying. Fraying is when threads pull off of the cut edge of a piece of cloth, making the edge look rough and unfinished.

Fabric glue is a special kind of white glue you can buy at fabric stores or craft stores. Look for a label that says "permanent" or "washable." Then you'll know it won't wash out after it's dry. Use it to glue fabric pieces together, and to attach ribbon, lace, sequins, and glitter.

Paints. You can use several kinds of paint to make clothes fun. *Fabric paint* is specially made for this purpose. There are many kinds of fabric paint, including glitter paint, which is sparkly, and puff paint, which puffs up high when you heat it. Always follow the directions on the fabric paint label.

You can also paint on clothes with *latex house paint*. It's especially good for drizzling (see page 12). Most kinds of *acrylic paint* are permanent, too, meaning they won't wash out. Test them on scrap fabric before you use them on a garment.

Most kinds of fabric paint are *nontoxic*, which means they are very safe. They will have "nontoxic" on their label. Other paints do not say "nontoxic," which means they could be harmful. *Always get permission* to use fabric paint before you begin. The same goes for dyes and permanent markers.

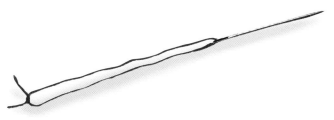

Thread. Regular sewing thread is strong enough for all the projects in this book. Use a double thickness and your thread will be even stronger. To make your thread double thick, cut a long piece of thread, and push one end through the eye (hole) of a needle. Pull the two ends together and tie them in a knot. It will look like a big loop of thread. Be careful when using a sharp needle!

Use *embroidery floss* for bigger stitches and for decoration (see Towel Tricks, page 34). Embroidery floss is made up of six little threads. You can pull them apart and use two or three instead of all six if you want.

Tennie Ties

Jazz up your tennis shoes with fancy shoelaces. Stripes, spots and colorful designs are easy to make with paint or markers.

You must use permanent ink markers to color on shoelaces. Regular water-based felt pens will "bleed" when they get wet and could ruin your shoes. *Be careful*—permanent ink markers have a strong, bad smell. *Always get permission* and use them outside or next to an open window. Wear old clothes and work on scrap paper or newspaper.

Shoelaces

Latex housepaint

Materials needed:

Permanent ink markers

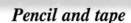

Pencil and tape

Stick

Fabric paint

Making Stripes. Paint or draw stripes on one side—make them fat or thin, straight or slanted. When it's dry, match the colors on the other side. Try glitter paint!

Fast Stripes. Wind your shoelace tight around a pencil. Tape both ends down to hold it in place. Paint or draw long stripes of color. Leave the inside plain.

Drizzle Laces. Lay a shoelace on newspaper. Drizzle it with latex housepaint. Let it dry for one hour; then drizzle the other side.

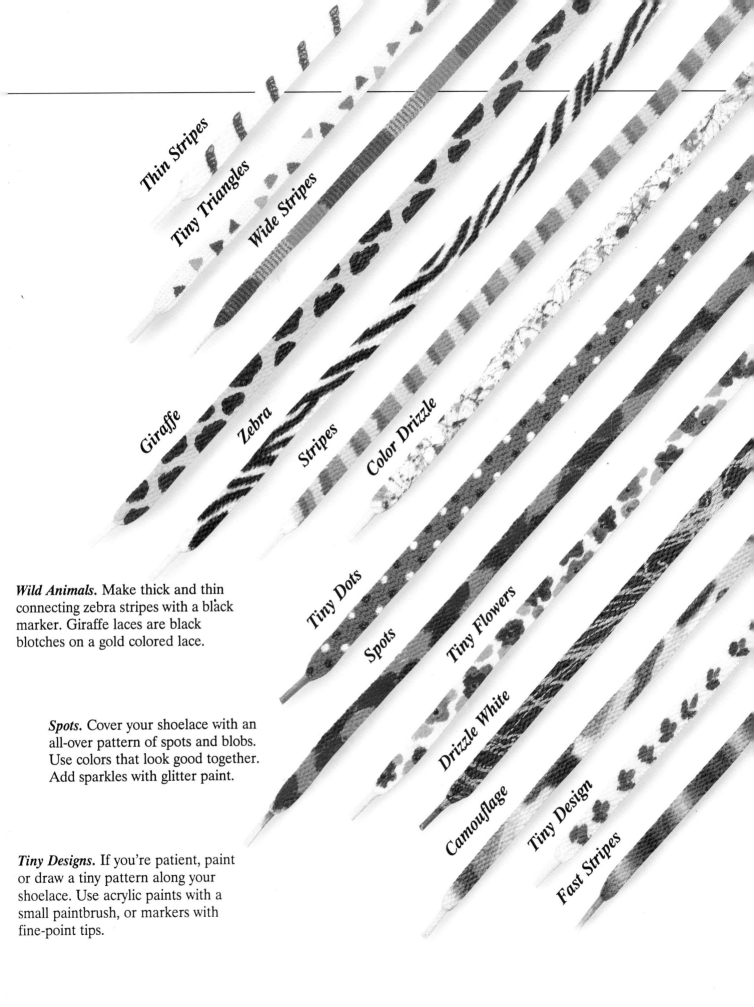

Thin Stripes

Tiny Triangles

Wide Stripes

Giraffe

Zebra

Stripes

Color Drizzle

Tiny Dots

Spots

Tiny Flowers

Drizzle White

Camouflage

Tiny Design

Fast Stripes

Wild Animals. Make thick and thin connecting zebra stripes with a black marker. Giraffe laces are black blotches on a gold colored lace.

Spots. Cover your shoelace with an all-over pattern of spots and blobs. Use colors that look good together. Add sparkles with glitter paint.

Tiny Designs. If you're patient, paint or draw a tiny pattern along your shoelace. Use acrylic paints with a small paintbrush, or markers with fine-point tips.

9

Painting T-Shirts

You can paint T-shirts, sweats and other clothes and turn them into colorful works of art. You'll learn several methods including drizzling or splattering paint for a wild look, or using stencils for a more careful design. Any way you choose is easy and fun and lets you express yourself on the clothes you wear!

Latex housepaint

Acrylic paint mixed with water

Materials needed:

Scrap paper, newspaper, and tracing paper

Scissors

Fabric paint

Sponge pieces

Toothbrush

Masking tape

Paintbrush

Get Ready

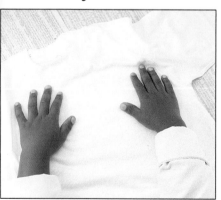

1 For drizzle, drop, and splatter, put the shirt in the bottom of a big cardboard box or on newspapers. If you don't use a box, wear old clothes!

2 Practice drizzling, dropping, and splattering paint on scrap cloth or newspaper before you work on good clothes.

3 If you use a new shirt, wash and dry it before you begin. Stuff layers of newspaper inside, and cover the neckband with paper and masking tape.

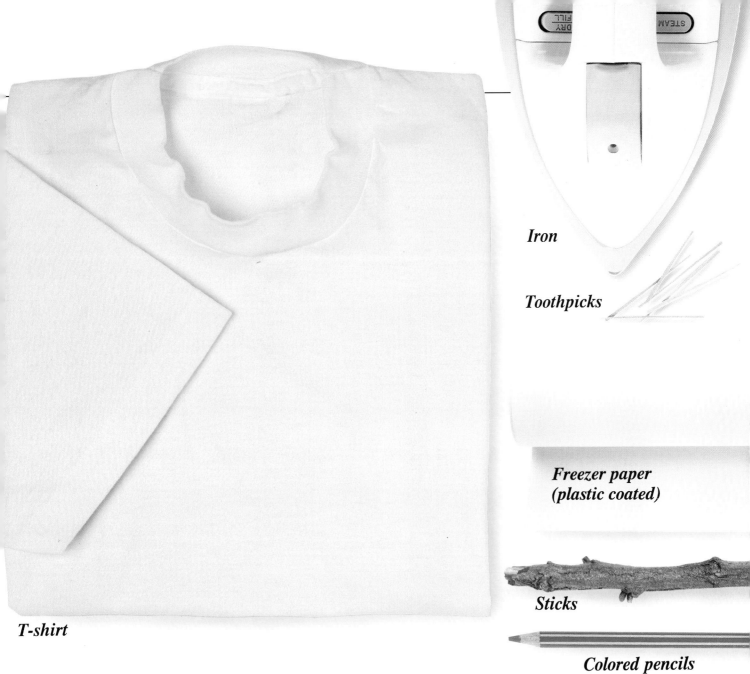

Iron

Toothpicks

*Freezer paper
(plastic coated)*

Sticks

Colored pencils

T-shirt

Drizzle

1 Dip a stick into latex paint. Pull it out and let it drip into the can for a moment. Then shake it gently over the shirt so the paint falls in a wiggly line.

2 Drizzle all over—even on the sleeves. Use cne color or several colors. Let it dry for three hours, then drizzle the back of the shirt the same way.

Drip drop. Mix acrylic paints with enough water to make them runny like syrup. Use toothpicks to drip drops of paint all over the shirt.

Drizzle and Splat T-Shirts

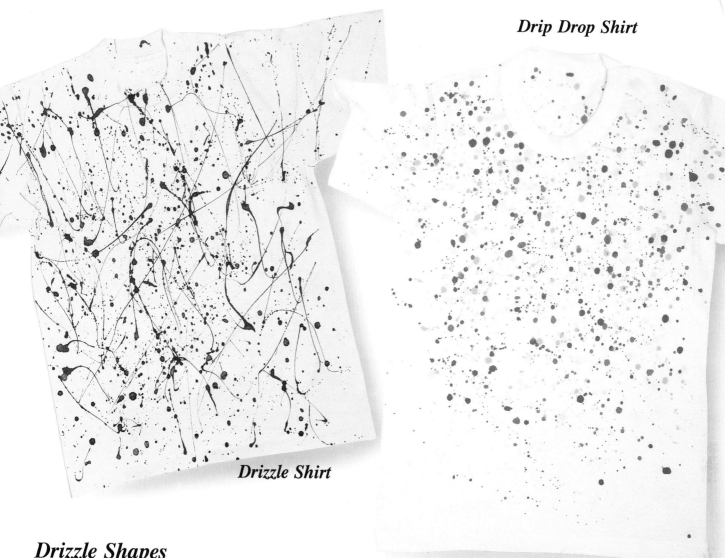

Drip Drop Shirt

Drizzle Shirt

Drizzle Shapes

1 Cut a simple shape out of a big piece of paper. Hearts and stars, circles and fat letters are easy to start with.

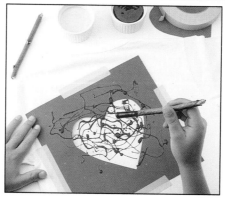

2 Tape the paper stencil on the top of the shirt. Drizzle paint through the hole onto the shirt. Carefully lift the stencil to see your design below.

3 You can make several stencil shapes on one shirt—use different colors for each one! Let each layer of paint dry before putting a new stencil on top.

Drizzle Stencil

Splatter Stencil

Get permission to make drizzle shoes! If the shoes aren't cloth, have an adult help you use fingernail polish or model airplane paint.

Night Sky Stencil

1 Make a horizon stencil. Cut mountain shapes in a large piece of paper and tape it to cover the bottom half of your shirt.

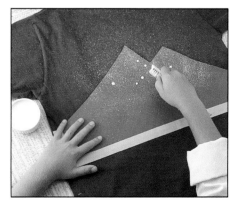

2 Dip an old toothbrush into white acrylic paint thinned with water. Rub your thumb across the bristles to splatter tiny flecks of paint all over the shirt.

3 Add flecks of light colors or glitter paint if you wish. Paint a thin crescent moon or cross-shaped stars. Let your shirt dry and remove the stencil.

Easy Stencil T-Shirts

Snowflake Stencil

Sun Stencil

Iron-On Shapes

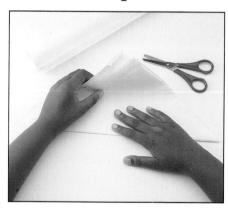

1 To make a snowflake stencil, fold a large piece of freezer wrap in half, and then in half again. Now fold that to make a triangle.

2 Use scissors to round the top. Cut zigzag or lacy holes down each side — but don't cut all the way across! Cut off the point and unfold the paper.

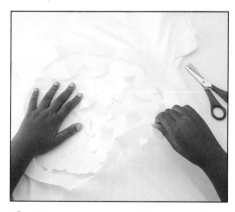

3 Place your snowflake stencil shiny side down on your T-shirt. Have an adult help you iron it in place. Remember to put newspaper or freezer paper inside the shirt.

Word Stencil

Name Stencil

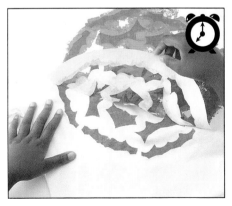

4 Put a little bit of latex or acrylic paint on a paper plate. With a sponge, dab the paint onto the cloth that shows through the holes in your stencil.

5 If you use more than one color, paint each color carefully with a different sponge piece. Let the paint dry completely, then pull off the stencil.

Iron-On Words. Sketch a word or a name on the dull side of the freezer paper. Cut out the letters and iron the stencil onto your shirt. Follow Steps 3, 4 and 5.

Picture Stencil T-Shirts

1 Draw a picture on regular paper. Draw something that has interesting shapes, and use lots of colors in the different shapes.

2 Make your first stencil: Trace your drawing onto the dull side of a piece of freezer paper. Cut out all the shapes you want to be the same color.

3 Have an adult iron the stencil in place. Dab on the paint. Let it dry (use a hairdryer to speed up drying time). Pull up the stencil.

If you paint on a dark garment, use several coats of paint with each stencil so the color of the garment doesn't show through.

Cut stencils of simple shapes to make an abstract design. Let each color dry completely. The shapes can overlap if you wish.

4 Put a new piece of freezer paper over your first drawing. Make a second stencil: Trace your drawing and cut out the shapes of your second color.

5 Lay this new stencil in place on top of what has already been painted on the shirt. Have an adult help you iron it down, then paint in the second color.

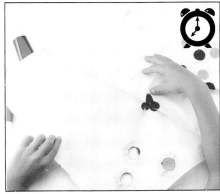

6 Let it dry, and peel up the stencil. Do this again and again for each color you want to use until you've painted the whole picture on the shirt.

Button Designs

Create a picture or design with colorful buttons. It's easy to glue or sew them on. They look best on plain, colored fabric. For light-weight clothes like T-shirts, use small buttons. Heavy things like denim, sweats and shoes can support bigger buttons. Turn your Buttons garment inside out when you wash it.

Materials needed:

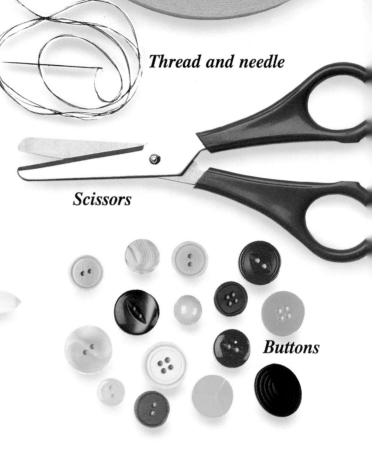

Masking tape

Thread and needle

Fabric paint

Scissors

Fabric glue

Buttons

Plan a design by laying buttons on your garment and moving them around until you like what you see. Then use tape to hold them in place.

Sew. You can sew the buttons on (ask an adult for help if you need it). Lift the tape from each button as you're ready to sew it in place.

Glue. You can glue the buttons in place with fabric paint! Make a ring of paint for each button to sit in, and the color will show around the edges.

If your buttons are close together, you can move from button to button (inside the garment) without tying a knot. If your buttons are far apart, sew each one by itself. Start with a knot in your thread. After you've stitched a button, use the needle to tie a knot on the inside of the garment. Cut the thread, and make a new knot for the next button.

This butterfly was painted with black and blue fabric paint. The buttons on top make him bright and colorful.

Show Your Spirit

Support your favorite team or club—make a colorful felt patch! Design an *insignia*, or badge, for your team using your school colors or a picture of your team mascot. You can sew or glue patches on jackets, sweatshirts, gym bags or banners.

There are many kinds of fancy letters to choose from. A few styles are shown at right—try them out, or make up your own.

Materials needed:

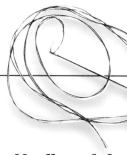
Needle and thre

Fabric paint

Felt

Colored pencils

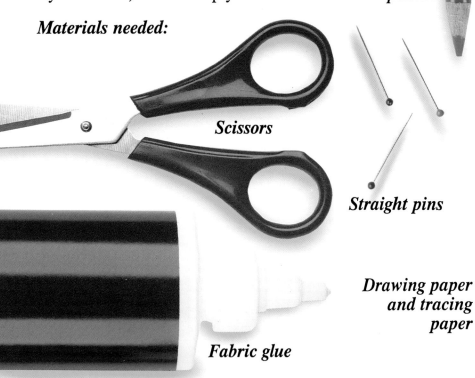

Scissors

Straight pins

Drawing paper and tracing paper

Fabric glue

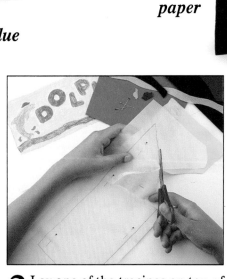

1 Plan your design on paper. Draw it as big as you want the patch to be. Make a tracing of each letter and shape in your drawing.

2 Lay one of the tracings on top of felt. Hold the paper in place with straight pins. Use it as a pattern to cut out the letters and shapes.

3 Cut out all the pieces. Then put them together following your design. Spread glue all over the back of each piece. Glue them down one at a time.

AABCDEFGHI
JKKLMNOPQ
RRSTUVWXYZ

ABCDEFGHIJKLMN
OPQRSTUVWXYZ

ABCDEFGHIJKLM
NOPQRSTUVWXYZ

4 Instead of cutting out the tiny inside of a letter, you can cut the shape of the hole out of the background color. Glue the hole shape *on top of* the letter.

5 Use fabric paint to draw on your patch. Add details and highlights with light colors. Be very careful, because you can't change it if you make a mistake!

6 If you put your patch on a garment you will wash, have an adult help you sew around each piece of your patch. Then sew the patch onto your garment.

Team Spirit

Once you design an insignia, like this one for a swim team called the Dolphins, you can use it over and over again on banners, caps and T-shirts.

This design was painted on a white iron-on patch with fabric paint. The paint comes in a tube with a small opening so it's easy to draw with. Iron-on patches are available at fabric and craft stores.

Here's a design for an art club, glued onto a tote bag for art supplies!

Soda Straw Weavings

Weave beautiful, colorful belts and things on a "loom" you make yourself. It's easy! Best of all, your woven creations will look so good, no one will believe you made them with soda straws!

Yarn

Materials needed:

6 plastic straws

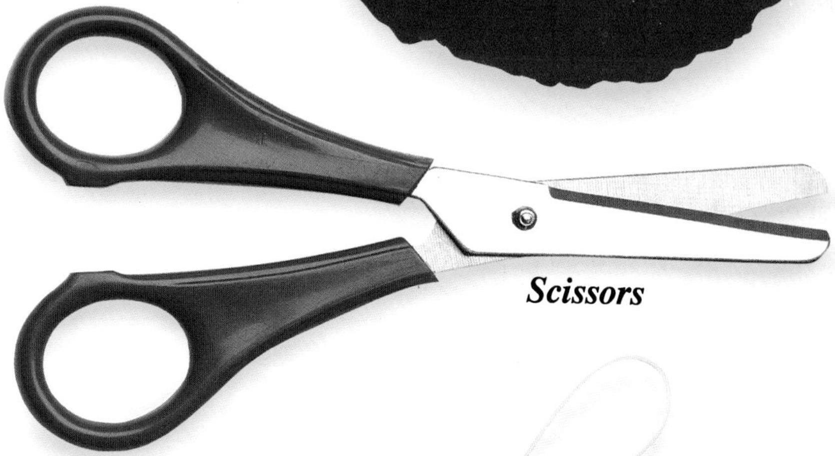

Scissors

Ruler

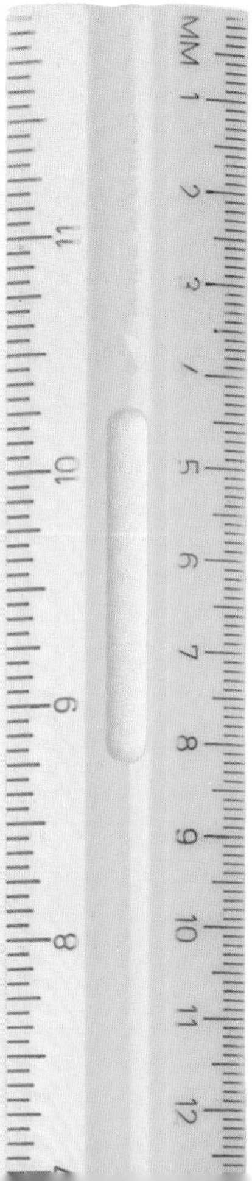

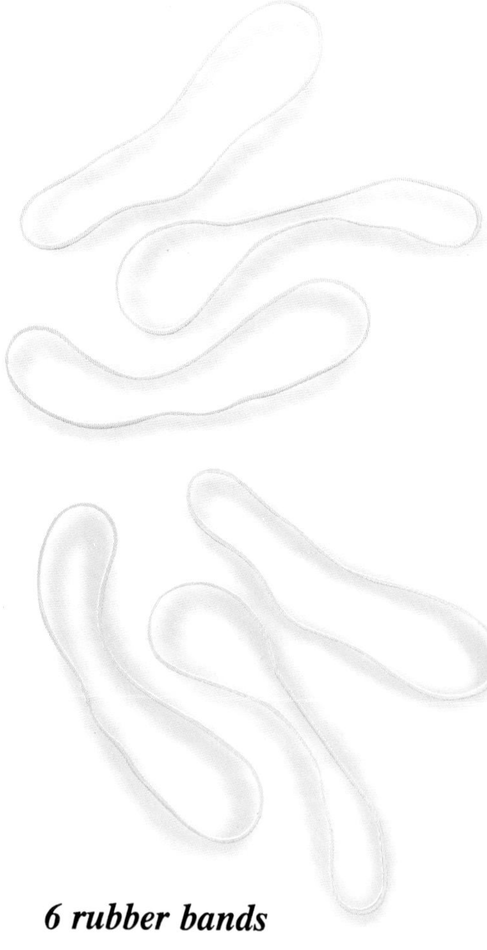

6 rubber bands

1 Cut six pieces of yarn 3′ (1 m) long. These are called *warp* strings. Tie them together in a knot at one end—a starting knot.

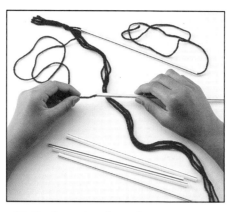

2 Push a plastic soda straw onto each warp string, right up to the starting knot.

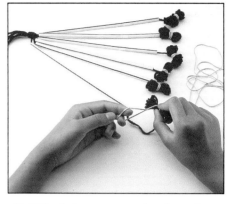

3 Wind the extra string hanging out of the end of each straw into a little ball and wrap it with a rubber band.

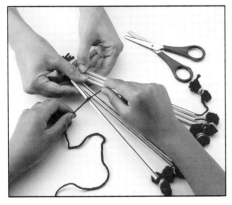

4 Cut another long piece of yarn—your *weaving* yarn. Tie one end onto one of the straws. Have someone help you hold the six straws in a row.

5 Start wrapping the weaving yarn over and under the straws. Weave around the last straw and back to where you started. Keep weaving back and forth.

6 When you get near the end of the piece of weaving yarn, tie another long piece of yarn onto it and keep weaving. Change colors if you wish.

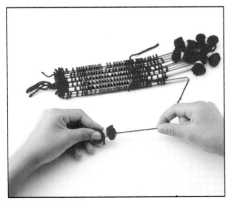

7 As the straws fill up, pull some of the yarn out of the balls at the ends of the warp strings.

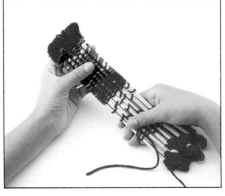

8 Push the woven part up onto the warp strings. Pull the straws down farther onto the yarn you pulled out of the balls. Then, weave some more.

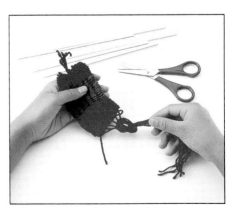

9 When you're finished weaving, tie the weaving yarn in a knot around one of the straws. Slip the straws off and tie an ending knot with all the warp strings.

Wearing Weavings

Ear Warmer

Tie a starting knot leaving 10″ of "tassle" hanging off the end of the knot. Weave until you have a strip long enough to fit over your head from ear to ear. Tie an ending knot leaving 10″ of tassle beyond the knot. Braid both tassles. Tie the braided ends behind your head under your hair.

Scarf

Dress up your doll or teddy bear! Start with warp strings as long as you want your scarf to be. Then weave the scarf and tie pretty tassles on each end.

Sash

Start with warp strings long enough to go around your waist plus several inches. Weave a long sash—it may take a couple of days to finish. Make a tassle at each end and tie the sash around your waist.

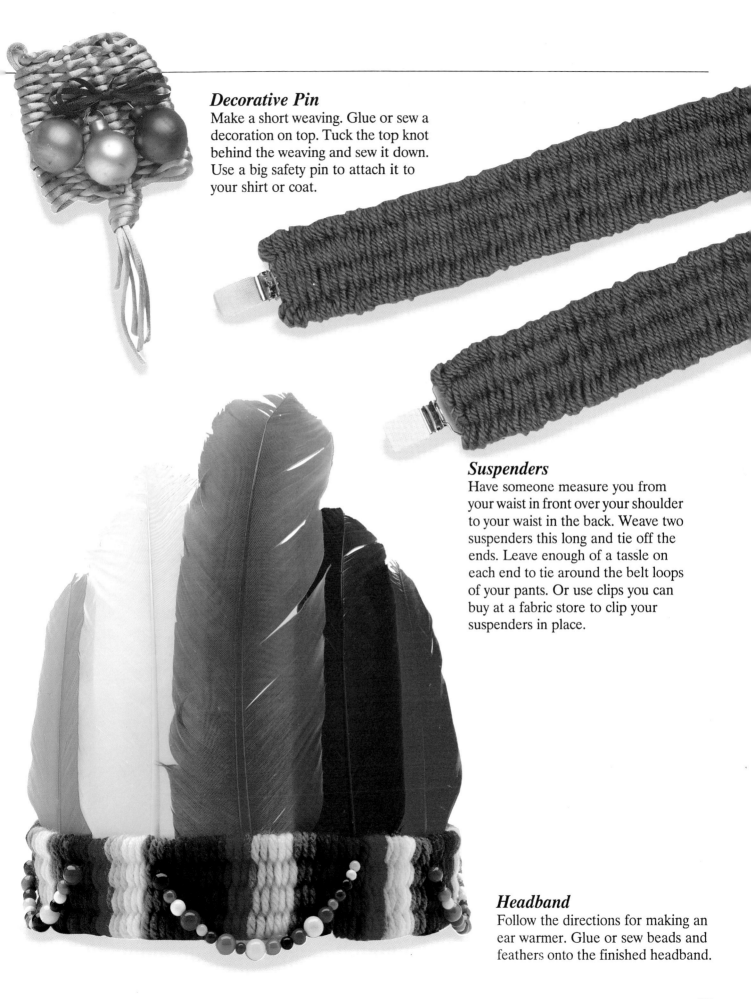

Decorative Pin
Make a short weaving. Glue or sew a decoration on top. Tuck the top knot behind the weaving and sew it down. Use a big safety pin to attach it to your shirt or coat.

Suspenders
Have someone measure you from your waist in front over your shoulder to your waist in the back. Weave two suspenders this long and tie off the ends. Leave enough of a tassle on each end to tie around the belt loops of your pants. Or use clips you can buy at a fabric store to clip your suspenders in place.

Headband
Follow the directions for making an ear warmer. Glue or sew beads and feathers onto the finished headband.

Critter Caps

Did you ever want to wear an alligator on your head? You can turn an old baseball hat into almost any animal. Start by choosing an animal to make. Look at pictures in wildlife books and magazines. You'll need to build the eyes, nose (or beak), ears, and horns if your animal has them. Use heavy paper, paper plates, or cardboard tubes. Decorate them with cut paper and fabric scraps. (You can buy the green foam for the alligator at craft stores.)

Once you put them together, you can't wash your critter caps. So wear them only on special days. When they wear out, pull the pieces off and use the hats to make new animals!

Old baseball cap

Materials needed:

Glue

Scissors

Decorations

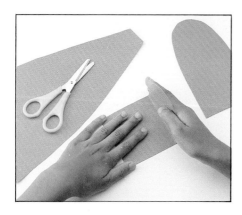

1 Cut a long triangle nose and two long rounded eye pieces out of heavy paper. Fold the rounded pieces in half so they'll stand up like the letter L.

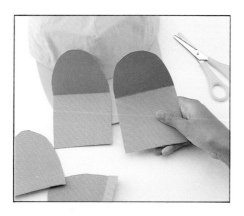

2 Hold the pieces up to the hat to see how they look. You may have to cut several test pieces until you get the size and shape you want.

3 Trace the paper pieces on the foam. Make the foam triangle bigger than the paper one. Cut the foam pieces out and glue them onto the paper.

Felt or fabric scraps

Green foam

Light cardboard

Felt pen

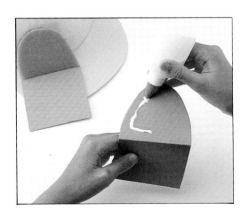

4 Glue the eyes onto the front of the cap so the bottom, flat part of the L lays on the cap's brim.

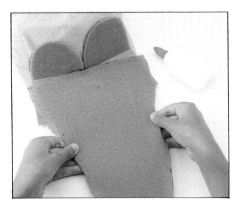

5 Glue the triangle nose onto the brim. Roll the sides of the foam under and glue them to the bottom of the paper to make a rounded lip.

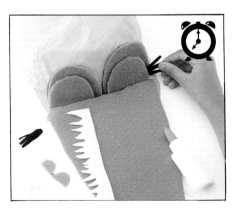

6 Add details: wiggly eyes, half-circle eyelids, felt teeth and eyelashes, half-circles of foam for nostrils, and anything else you think of. Let it dry overnight.

Critter Caps

Duck Cap

Dog Cap

Sheep Cap

Rabbit Cap

Alligator Cap

31

Towel Tops

Wear a work of art to the beach, pool, or any time you want to lounge around in style. Or, make an apron, tote bag or baby bib. After you sew your towel together, it's fun to stitch a picture on the front with colorful *embroidery*. If you've never sewn or embroidered before, ask an adult to help you.

Materials needed:

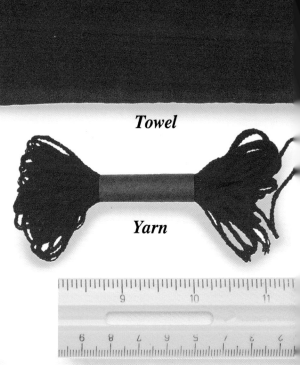

Embroidery floss and needle

Scissors

Towel

Yarn

Double wide bias tape

Ruler

How to Sew

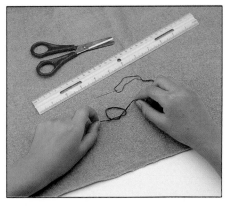

1 Cut a piece of thread about 24″ (72 cm) long and poke it through the eye of a needle. Pull the ends even and tie a knot.

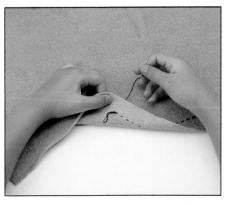

2 Sew with small stitches in and out of your fabric. Check each stitch to be sure your thread hasn't tangled underneath.

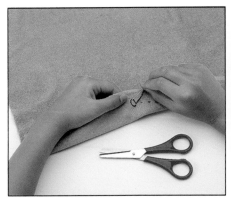

3 After you've stitched for a while, the thread will begin to get short. Push the needle to the back of your work, make a knot and cut the thread.

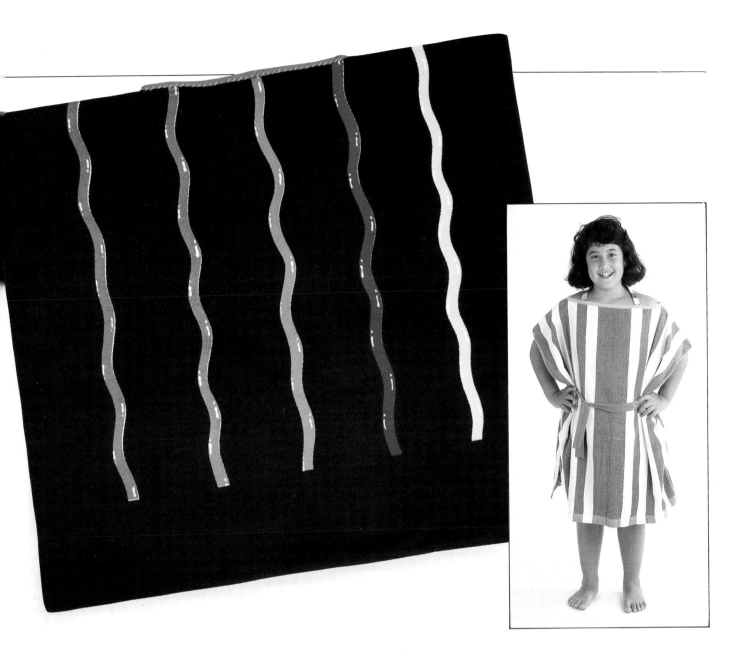

Make a Top

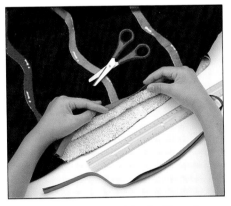

1 Fold your towel in half and cut a 9″ (27 cm) slit in the middle of the fold. Cut a 19″ (57 cm) piece of bias tape and cover the cut edge with it.

2 Cut off a long piece of embroidery floss and thread it through the needle. Make a knot at the end. Begin sewing, in and out, through the towel and bias tape.

3 Make a knot when you're done and cut off the extra floss. Sew up the sides of the towel the same way, leaving 12″ (36 cm) from the fold for arm holes.

Towel Tricks

You can make fancy borders on your Towel Tops by stitching along the edges. Make rows of chain stitches, or lines of different colored running stitches. Stitch a picture with cross-stitch. Plan your design on paper first. Then draw right on the towel with a pencil or chalk—the lines will wash out in the laundry.

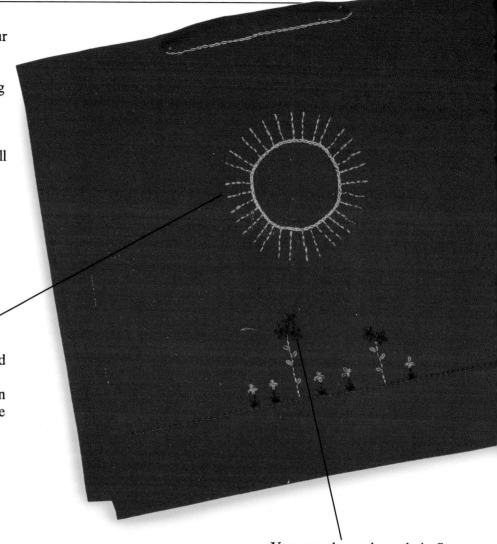

This sun was stitched with chain stitches and running stitches. To end a chain of chain stitches, bring the needle up inside your last loop. Then push it back into the cloth near where the needle came up, but on the *outside* of the loop. Make a knot in the back of the towel and trim the thread.

You can also make a chain flower. Make several chain stitches, going around in a circle, all starting at the same point.

Running Stitch

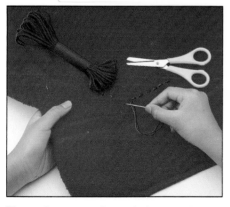

To make a running stitch, you simply sew in and out in a straight line. Be careful to make the stitches the same size and the same distance apart.

Cross-Stitch

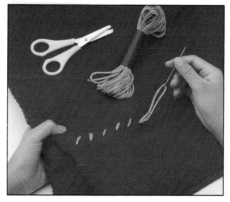

1 Cross-stitch uses little X shapes to color in big areas. Make a row of slanted lines going up from left to right.

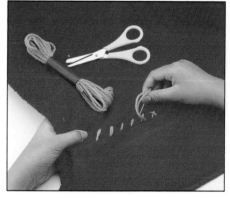

2 Now go back in the other direction, finishing each X by making a slanted line up from right to left.

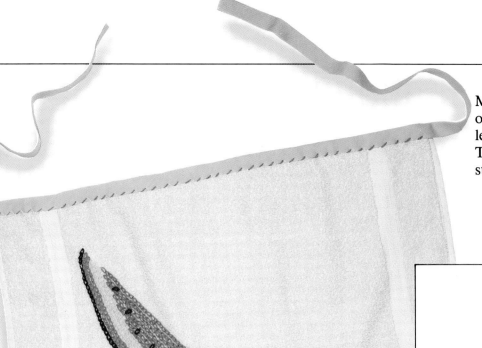

Make an apron! Sew bias tape along one long side of a towel leaving long lengths on both ends to be the ties. This watermelon is made of chain stitches.

Make a baby bib! Cut a half-circle for the neck and line it with bias tape, leaving long lengths on both ends to be the ties. This one is decorated with cross-stitches.

Chain Stitch

1 Bring the needle up from underneath the towel. Then push it back in, right next to where you came up.

2 Leave a loop of yarn setting on top of the towel. Bring the needle up from underneath again, inside the loop you just made!

3 Push the needle in right next to where you came up. Leave another loop setting on top of the towel. Make a long chain of loops.

35

Cloth Collage

Make beautiful pictures and abstract designs with cloth scraps, fabric glue and paint. Turn them into wall hangings or fun things to wear!

Materials needed:

Scissors

Fabric paint

Fabric scraps

Fabric glue

Decorations

1 Cut pieces of fabric to make an abstract pattern or a picture of a real thing. Arrange the pieces until you get a design you like.

2 Lift the cut pieces one at a time, spread glue on the back, and set them in place. Glue the edges down well. Wash your hands often.

3 Outline the cut pieces with puffy fabric paint — it looks great, and holds them tight. Lay your finished collage flat to dry overnight.

When your collage is dry, make a hem by folding the edges over and gluing them to the back. Put a stick in the top hem and attach a ribbon to make a wall hanging.

Your cloth collage must be sturdy enough to go through the washing machine if you are going to wear it. Make sure you glue all the edges down and seal them with puffy paint.

37

Jacket Jazz

Dress up your jackets with colorful decorations. Here are twelve things to try (from here to page 43). Read through all the directions before you begin—you may need special tools or supplies. Always plan your whole design and practice on scraps before you work on your good clothes.

Materials needed (in addition to a denim jacket):

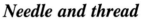

Needle and thread

Fabric paint

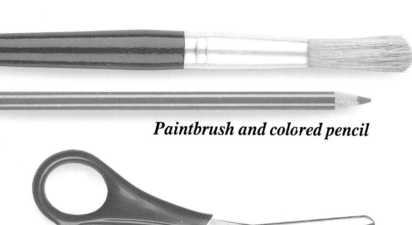

Paintbrush and colored pencil

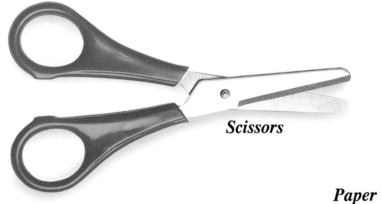

Scissors

Decorations

Paper

Fabric glue

Painted fish and glitter

Star stencils and graffiti

Paint it. Draw a picture or pattern with a colored pencil, then color it in with fabric paint. Use lots of paint.

Graffiti. Draw block letters with a pencil, then fill in colors with fabric paint. Write your name, initials, or a funny saying.

Stencils. Cut a simple shape out of heavy paper. Trace it on your jacket with a colored pencil. Carefully color each one with fabric paint.

Jacket Fringe

Bangles. Have an adult help you sew on plastic paperclips, charms, or buttons that hang down.

Beads. Put sparkly beads onto safety pins. Hook six or seven beaded pins together with one safety pin. Sew a row of these across your jacket.

1 ***Fringe.*** Cut strips of T-shirt material, felt or suede to fit under pocket flaps or along the bottom of the sleeves.

2 Have an adult help you sew on the cloth. Cut up into the cloth, but not all the way to the top. Tie on beads if you wish.

1 ***Studs.*** You can buy studs at fabric stores. There are kits to help you attach them (and jewels and coins!). Or, carefully poke them through the cloth by hand.

2 Turn the jacket over to the inside where the pointy ends of the studs poke through. Use a wooden spoon to bend them back against the fabric.

Paper clip bangles
with painted centers

Studs and beaded
safety pins

Painted zebra pattern
and felt fringe

41

Jacket Fluff

Ribbon and Lace. Attach ribbon, rickrack (zigzag cloth trim) and lace to your jacket with fabric glue. Follow the instructions on the fabric glue.

Glitter. Paint a picture or design on your jacket with fabric glue or fabric paint. Sprinkle glitter on it while the glue is wet. Let it dry overnight.

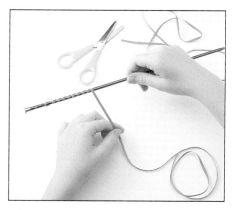

1 **Ribbon Curls.** Tightly wrap a metal knitting needle with cloth ribbon. Tie the ribbon around the needle at both ends. Soak it in water for a few minutes.

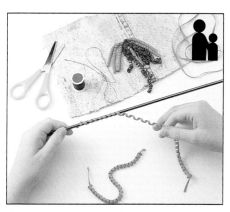

2 Have an adult help you "bake" it in a 250° F oven for an hour. When it's cool, unwind it and sew the curls to your jacket in bunches.

1 **Rag Puffs.** Use *pinking shears* to cut narrow strips of cloth. The shears make a zigzag edge that keeps the cloth from fraying.

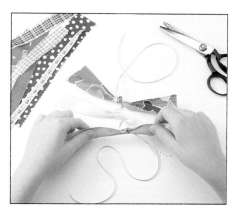

2 Cut the strips 7″ (21 cm) long. Tie the strips in knots around a 9″ (27 cm) piece of thin ribbon.

3 Tie the ribbon in a tight knot to gather the cloth strips into a puffy pompon. Have an adult help you sew the pompon to your jacket.

Glitter and rickrack

Rag puffs

Tie-Dye T-Shirts

Tie a shirt up with string or rubber bands and dye it with fabric dye—*tie-dye!* Learn other methods using paper clips or a spray bottle. You can design lots of great shirts.

Be careful. The best place to tie-dye is outdoors on a warm day. If you work indoors, work over a sink and be very careful of drips and spills. Wear rubber gloves and old clothes.

Mixing fabric dyes: Buy dye at any supermarket. Have an adult help you mix a spoonful of dye with 2 cups of hot water in a bucket or glass jar.

Materials needed:

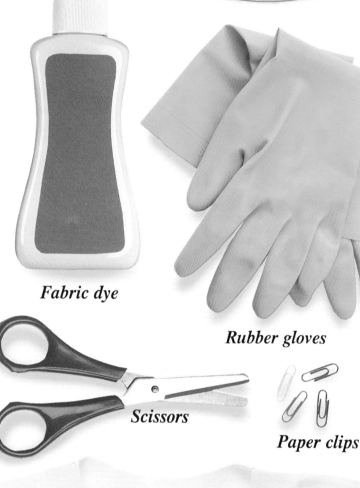

Bucket and hot water

Fabric dye

Rubber gloves

Waxed paper

Scissors

Paper clips

Paintbrush

Plastic spoons

T-shirt

String

Rubber bands

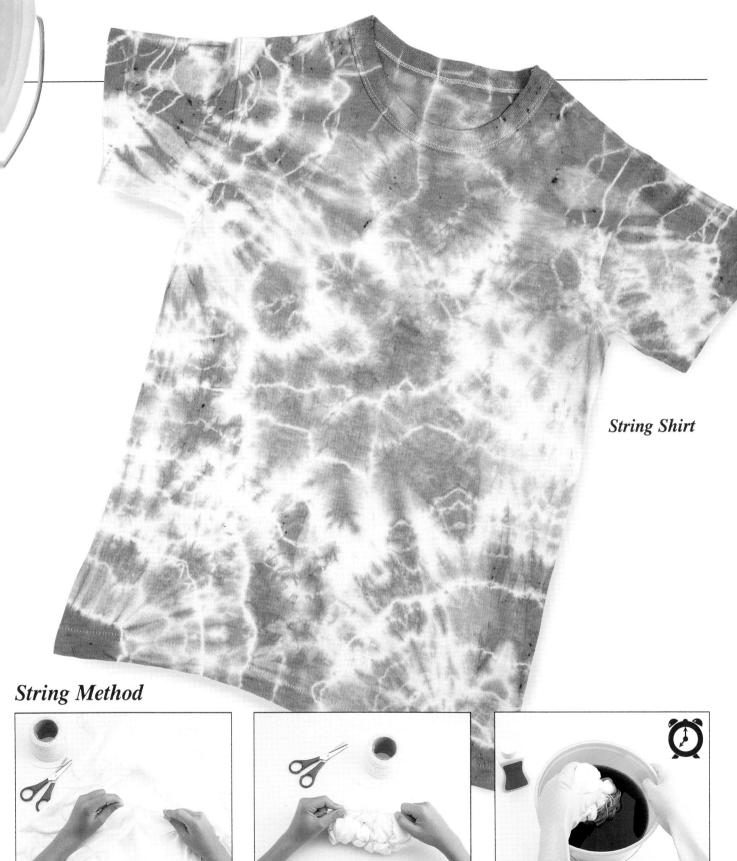

String Shirt

String Method

1 Tie a long piece of sturdy string onto a bottom corner of the T-shirt. Make it tight.

2 Crumple the shirt, wrapping the string *tightly* around the shirt as you crumple. Crumple and wrap the whole shirt and tie a knot.

3 Dip the shirt into dye for one minute. Let it set in the sink or out on the grass for a half hour before you undo the string.

Tie-Dye Tricks

Rubber Band Shirt

Rubber Band Method

Bull's-Eye
Poke up one big peak in the middle of the shirt. Wrap three rubber bands around it. Drip a different color into each section.

1 Poke up little peaks all over a T-shirt. Wrap each one with two rubber bands. Make them very tight.

2 Make three colors of dye. Use a spoon to carefully drip one color on the tip of each peak.

3 Drip a second color into the middle section of each peak. Drip a third color onto the body of the shirt. Let it set for a half hour. Undo the rubber bands.

Crumple a T-shirt into a long roll. Wrap string or rubber bands around the roll. Drip two colors of dye on it and let it set for a half hour.

Paper Clip Method

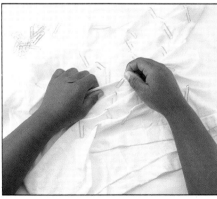

1 Lay a T-shirt flat and place sheets of waxed paper inside. Pinch up rows of folds across the front of the shirt. Use paper clips to hold them up.

2 Dip a paintbrush into dye and paint the top edges of the folds. Work slowly and let the dye soak into the cloth.

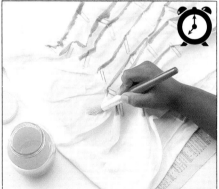

3 With a second color, paint a big sun in the corner and sunrays between the folds. Let the shirt dry completely before you take the waxed paper out.

Tie-Dye Pictures

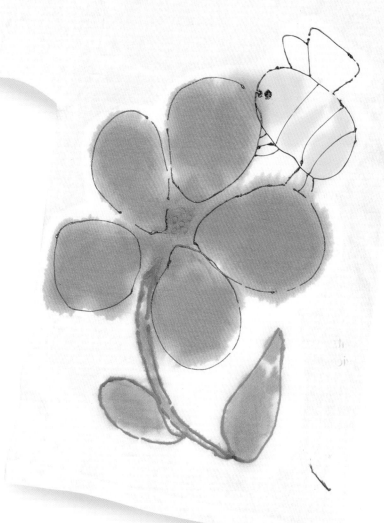

Freehand flower and bumble bee. Draw over your picture with fabric paints like puffy paint or glitter paint. They come in squeeze bottles so they're easy to draw with.

Freehand Method

1 Lay a T-shirt flat and put waxed paper inside. Make a big flower with a spoon or paintbrush. Work slowly—let the dye spread out.

2 Cut waxed paper shapes to cover your flower. Pour another color of dye into a spray bottle.

3 Put the shirt in a big box or outside on the grass. Spray dye on the T-shirt all around your flower. Let it dry completely.